Own Your Outcomes

Pat Semeraro

ISBN:1547046074
ISBN-13:9781547046072

ACKNOWLEDGEMENTS

Special thanks (that can never be put into words!) to my wife Cristin who lived through the jobs, minute by minute, and day by day, that eventually became some of the stories and wisdom in this book. Thanks decades earlier to my parents who drove me to jobs when I was too young to drive myself, for letting me build speakers in their garage, for letting me park a full size box truck in their driveway… Thanks to Dusty Rollins for the encouragement to write this book. Thanks to the PTE Productions family for the opportunities to dream, learn, and eventually, get some of this stuff right. Thanks to my amazing colleagues at Universal Orlando who continue to be an inspiration even today. And thanks to the greater powers of the universe that have endowed me with the imagination, time and space to try and to fail, and to try again, as I practiced this interesting craft we call show business.

CONTENTS

Who Should Read This Book?

If you happened to observe a jogger, who was about to run over the edge of a cliff, what would you do? Would you whisper to them from a distance being extra careful to not ruin their vibe? Would you gesture subtly to them they might possibly be on the wrong course or suggest in a passive-aggressive manner they *might* want to *maybe* change direction, while being extra careful to not make them upset or bruise their ego?

Or would you scream at the top of your lungs HEEEEEEYYYYYYYYYYYY!!!!!!!!!!!! while running full speed ahead and lunging at the person's ankles to save them from going over the cliff?

Parts of writing this book have felt like how I image that moment would play out, of screaming at the top of my lungs while lunging at someone's ankles. It's not my place to worry about temporarily offending a person's sensibilities if I can help save their life.

In the world of meetings and events, if there's even a possibility that I can save someone's job, or save a non-profit money, or save someone from stress, or embarrassment, or any of the bad things that happen when meetings or events go terribly wrong, then I will scream (and hope that you would do the same for me!).

Human to human, I'm personally grateful to you for the opportunity to share these thoughts and ideas. If this book challenges your assumptions, good! If we as an industry and community, (providers and buyers) continue to do the same things we've always done, there is a real possibility that we'll get the same things we've always gotten.

In this world, there are countless guides, seminars, classes and training about how to "sell" better, how to "close" more effectively, how to "upsell" and more. Typically, with a promise of great riches if that particular strategy is implemented correctly and with the right "hustle" and attitude.

This book is a practical guide of how to buy better. As a buyer of A/V services, buying better and smarter will save you money. It is not full of "hot tips" or quickie listicles about how to beat up your vendor or "bend them over a barrel" or outsmart them into giving you the lowest possible price. You probably already know how to do that. Quite the opposite, this is about working together as counterparts, which begins with speaking the same language.

A language, I propose, neither side is speaking currently.

If you a meeting planner or event producer and currently having a conversation with one of the top A/V providers, congratulations! You are now a part of their "selling system" and will be tracked by a computer through each step, all of it systematically designed to get you to a yes as quickly as possible while maximizing their profits. Despite how the focus-group developed, field-tested, continuously iterated sales language makes you feel comfortable and confident in their abilities, the equity capital or "big money" behind the operation is not committed to maximizing YOUR value. You are a number on a spreadsheet, part of a monthly or yearly quota. And that may be your best case scenario.

What about the smaller "regional" or "Mom and Pop" operations that promise "boutique" service or highly personalized experiences. How do you know if they are competent or if they can even deliver on their promise?

Then there are the companies with outdated websites, poor quality marketing collateral, and few testimonials. If they can't even tell their own story, how are they going to tell yours?

If you are someone responsible for sourcing A/V services and don't know how and where to start, this book is for you. If you are a multi-decade industry veteran and frustrated with some of the choices the A/V industry has made and how those choices don't always look out for the best interests of your clients, this book is for you. If you are curious what goes on "behind the curtain" in the world of show business and how A/V can make or break a meeting or event, this book is for you.

If you believe that most providers are GOOD PEOPLE and genuinely want to give good value, and good service but find it frustrating that they speak a different language than you, then this book is a must read.

To all the amazing meeting and events professional throughout the world, let the record show that I believe the meetings and event industry is noble work. Anything that brings people together to meet, learn, collaborate, and be inspired, makes the world a better place. This is the work that you do; it's important and it matters. We also know that our real boss is the audience member, meeting attendee, and event guest. Let's together do whatever is necessary to ensure that they are treated to the best experience possible and that as "the help" you and I are effective, cognizant of our role and always humble and grateful for the gift of people's trust.

Intro (Sort of...)

We were less than 5 minutes from "doors" and the crowd in the lobby was rowdy. More than 200 feet away, from behind the thick drape backstage in the locked ballroom I could hear the sounds of chanting and anticipation. More than three thousand people from all across the United States had been looking forward to this night; a once a year celebration and inspiration.

I was a relatively new team member and was asked to jump in as the technical supervisor for this private event at a world-famous Orlando theme park.

The opening music was "cued up" (ready to start at the exact moment the doors would be flung open) the walk-in lighting look was set and looked amazing, four large video screens were scrolling the custom photo slide-show and the "show team" (technicians that operate the equipment during show) was in place and standing by.

A call came over the two-way radio from the manager in the lobby "Can we open doors a few minutes early? This group is READY TO GO!"

Then, in the next instant, time stopped. What's that smell I wondered? It kind of smells electrical... A quick scan across the dimly lit back-stage area and there it was; a small stream of smoke coming out of the electrical power distribution system.

Back to the radio, "switch to channel 3" (our private channel) "We just need a few more minutes to button up…" I calmly mentioned to the manager in the lobby. "Go back to channel one, I'll radio you when you can let everyone in."

SH*T!!!!!!!

In the next 60 seconds three technicians with flashlights verified the diagnosis that the electrical distribution system was gently smoldering. Fully live with electricity, we opened it up to look inside. One of the main power connections was glowing red hot and threatening to catch fire; we were minutes from the entire production going dark.

We always carry small AC fans in the workboxes, and this was their moment to come through in a crisis. With one technician holding the electrical rack door open, and another holding a light so we could see, it was like the game of operation as I very slowly and very carefully put the small running fan inside the electrical rack, pointed at the connection that was glowing red. This rack was "live" with HUNDREDS of amps of high-voltage current. One twitch, one slip, and I would be instantly dead.

With the fan installed and several technicians re-routing the electrical load, I calmly called the manager back on the radio and said "Let 'em in!"

That show was a success but it was a wake-up call for me and it should be a wake-up call for you too.

What actually goes on behind the scenes? How competent is the technical show team that you are entrusting with your event, your company's money, your guest's safety and your reputation? What is their training? Have they even slept in the past 48 yours? How good is your vendor's equipment? What is their safety record? Do they follow federal and local labor laws? Is your event the biggest show they've ever tried to tackle? What happens to you personally if everything at the event you're responsible for goes terribly wrong?

Join me in a behind-the-scenes look at corporate show business from the viewpoint of a multi-decade audio visual practitioner. You'll learn how to ask the right questions, quickly compare bids and quotes from multiple vendors, screen out the bad providers, and never pay too much.

Chapter 1

A/V, What the Heck Is it?

Product or Service? Skilled Trade, or Practice?

Why Should You Care?

Nobody thinks about (or cares about) A/V until they're forced to. You wake up one day and find yourself in charge of planning a company meeting, gala, or event. Who "deals with" the PowerPoint? The band just emailed you their "rider", your boss demanded you spend "as little as possible" and tomorrow you have a meeting scheduled with the "in-house" A/V Company. Now what?

It's difficult for me to imagine what that moment must feel like. How do you navigate that river? How do you know when vendors are being truthful? What audio visual support does your meeting, gala, or event REALLY need to be successful vs what the vendor is trying to "sell" you? Why do the quotes you receive look so different and vary so much in cost? Isn't a speaker just a speaker and a microphone just a microphone?

Let's take a step back and paint some lines with a wide brush. For the purposes of this book, audio visual refers to the "business" of providing stage lighting, sound systems, video screens, computers, projectors and TVs and making them all work together so a CEO can be heard perfectly when addressing his audience, the fundraiser PowerPoint makes everyone cry at just the right time and your company sales-kickoff hot-shot keynote speaker isn't standing in the dark during his presentation.

This business has many names, including Audio Visual, A/V, event staging, event production, show technology and more. Those names, while technically nuanced, are often used interchangeably and sometimes to great confusion. (Let's say you receive two quotes for your meeting. Company A is an Audio Visual Services provider and company B is an event Staging Company. Is there a difference? The answer is, it depends.)

Because A/V companies (like most businesses) like to make money, many times they will also offer stage decks and mobile stages, scenic design and fabrication, small and large format graphics, event drape, power generators, "from scratch" custom video content, PowerPoint slide development and graphics, and on and on.

Is an A/V company the best place to get the drape for your presentation or the generator for your outdoor party? That depends... Are those items part of their core competencies? Can they deliver when it counts just as well as a specialist can, and save you money at the same time? (That would be a win-win, right?) Knowing the right questions to ask can make all the difference between a stressful experience for you and questionable experience for your guests vs a smooth and fun experience for you and an amazing experience your guests.

Attempting to shop A/V as a product, (like renting a bounce house, for instance) sets you up for a tough journey and possibly worse. A/V is a practiced discipline but delivered as a service. As an industry that "grew up" organically, there are many ways to accomplish the same goals and how those goals are accomplished depends largely on the provider and the specific team on your event. Besides safety, there are no absolutes. Put five A/V experts in a room, and ask them a question, you might get seven different answers. (Some "experts" may not even agree with themselves!)

Most confusing of all, each of the seven answers might be correct.

It is easy to misinterpret A/V as a trade or shop it as a product. Much of the knowledge possessed by the industry is learned on the job, passed down verbally from journeymen to newbies and no licenses or formal training are required to practice A/V. (** see footnote regarding overhead rigging) Yet, how to "beautifully" light up a stage, what "sounds good" speaking into a microphone, and even understanding the steps of how to turn an idea into a show; these are expressions of art, open to interpretation and every event is an iteration (not a repeat) of all the ones that came before. The idea of A/V as a discipline and delivered as a service is something we'll build on in the following chapters.

How can you know if a provider is any good? And if by reputation they are known to be good, how do you know if they'll be any good for you and for your meeting or event?

You can start with certification. One certification exists, called CTS, (Certified Technology Specialist). This certification (which I hold) is recognized around the world and is based on a set of best practices which are grounded in rules, delivery formulas and guest safety. CTS certification should be your first question to any provider of A/V that you are considering entrusting with your event and your money. If your provider is CTS certified, you can be confident that they will look at your request from a known place of how to "get it done" effectively and safely. You will know that they meet a certain standard of competence.

Another recognized certification is ETCP for Entertainment Technician Certification Program. More tactical than CTS, this certification can be specialized in overhead rigging, portable power, or general entertainment technician. (ETCP Certification also helps technical managers and producers screen out the "less capable" when they are hiring the show team for your event.) ETCP holds safety and health as the first principal of its code of ethics and conduct.

Other principals include honesty, objective truthfulness, inclusion and diversity and more. As a meeting planner and or A/V buyer, these are qualities you should care about.

If you were about to undergo surgery, would you prefer a surgeon with no formal training, possibly making statements like *"Let's cut here and see what happens..."* or would you prefer someone with practical real-life experience that is also grounded in best practices which are vetted by the top experts from around the world?

If a provider is not certified, then how do you know that they know what they're doing? From a photo of someone else's event? Because they say they can? Is "word of mouth" enough to satisfy you that your money is being invested wisely and your guests will be safe?

If someone tells you they have "20 years of experience" is it your job to figure out if they truly have 20 years of experience or if they only have one year of experience repeated 20 times. Have they been doing the same thing, over and over, for years and years, while the rest of the industry has moved on?

ACTION STEPS you can use RIGHT NOW

(Applies to anyone involved with vetting and hiring an A/V vendor)

- *Ask A/V vendors what certifications they hold*
- *Ask A/V vendors about their internal training programs*
- *Ask A/V vendors about their safety record*
- *Ask A/V vendors how much insurance they carry. E & O or just liability?*
- *Ask A/V vendors how many events per year (that are similar to your event, not total!) they support*
- *Ask A/V vendors about typical obstacles they see on events like yours, and what they normally do to overcome those obstacles*

- *Ask A/V vendors what their "dream client" looks like*
- *Ask A/V vendors what are their core competencies? And what else do they also support outside of their core competencies that might be helpful to you?*

If you are someone who is uncomfortable asking those types of questions, then by all means delegate them to someone else to be the "bad cop" but before we go any further, let's get real. The variety of ways that you can spend too much, receive too little, get the wrong thing entirely and even put people's lives at risk, are truly astounding. From the largest companies to the smallest, any one of them can be the exact WRONG fit for your needs at any given moment.

Remember, YOU are the client; the vendors work for YOU, and it is their responsibility to try and earn and keep YOUR business, whatever that takes. For me personally, the tougher the questions a prospect or client asks, the more comfortable I am working with them and the more confident I become that their outcomes will be great.

Asking the RIGHT questions is the first step to OWNING YOUR OUTCOMES.

One exception is overhead rigging, (the practice of temporarily "hanging" equipment or décor from a ceiling or other structure) when it is provided by a reputable hotel, convention center or venue. The venue requires that anything hung overhead be done by their trained and certified riggers. This is a good thing! Incorrect and unsafe rigging can result in injury or death and venues have lots of great reasons to mandate that their people must be used to hang equipment over people's heads. Outside of venues is a different story and it is the provider's discretion on whether or not it uses certified riggers. Buyer beware!!

Pat Semeraro

Chapter 2

Great A/V is Often Invisible

Great A/V takes LOTS of work to not be noticed, both in planning and execution. Some of that work is your responsibility (in the planning phase) and the rest of that work is the job of your provider to plan and execute successfully.

One of the ironies about A/V support is that because its role is a supporting one, people only really notice it when something goes wrong. It's normal to hear guests make comments *like* **"Look at those flowers. They're beautiful!"** Never has any guest, ever, said **"Look at that microphone. It's beautiful!"** But, should that microphone quit working, now EVERYONE will notice it! It's all about doing certain things so a bunch of other things DON'T happen.

Let's flip the coin over. These are some of the things about A/V that people will notice.

- Squealing/squeaking microphones
- Stage lights that flicker or don't work
- Loose cords that people trip over
- Microphones that aren't turned on
- Video screens that are visually crooked
- Projectors that randomly quit
- Microphones that can't be heard clearly
- Anything on fire

- Projectors that display images with weird color tint, blurry images, flickering/unstable images, dim output,
- PowerPoint remotes that don't work
- Laptops that freeze up
- PowerPoint presentations with videos that stutter or get stuck
- The wrong video is started during a presentation
- Wireless microphones that make strange fizzing, whirring, static'y noises
- Anything that falls over

Great A/V support means invisible A/V support. You may never get credit or be praised for doing a great job with something that nobody notices. But you still have to do your best to make sure the A/V support is the correct solution and perfectly implemented in order to deliver the content flawlessly and on-cue. So that no one will notice.

This is not a bummer, it's an opportunity to step up where other people step aside or leave success to luck. It's an opportunity to deliver for your audience when others have let them down. It's an opportunity to OWN YOUR OUTCOMES.

ACTION STEPS you can use RIGHT NOW
(Applies to anyone involved with onsite managing a meeting or event)

- *NEVER be "OK" with equipment that doesn't work*
- *NEVER be "OK" with anything that looks unsafe or is unsafe*
- *NEVER be "OK" with loose or unsecured wires in the guest spaces*
- *NEVER be "OK" with incompetence*

Chapter 3

It's All About the Content

Let's say your favorite restaurant also caters and you happen to be throwing a party. Parties are fun and people love great food; placing your order should be a "piece of cake…"

Do you:

- Scenario A)
  - Rent 4 ovens from said restaurant (and try to negotiate the price of the ovens separately)
  - Rent 20 chef's knives from said restaurant (and try to negotiate the price of the knives separately)
  - Rent 30 pots and baking pans from said restaurant (and try to negotiate the price of the pots and pans separately)
  - Rent a "miscellaneous cookware package" from said restaurant (and try to negotiate the price of the cookware separately)
  - Rent 2 dishwashers from said restaurant (and try to negotiate the price of the dishwashers separately)
  - Rent electric power for the ovens and dishwashers for 10 hours
  - Hire one "lead" chef for 10 hours
  - Hire 6 "assist" chefs for 5 hours
  - Hire 4 miscellaneous kitchen laborers (for cleanup, etc.)
  - Purchase the following consumables
    - Serving trays
    - Water for cleaning

- Miscellaneous "spice and seasonings package"
  - o Ask if delivery of food to your party is free
  - o Actual menu is TBD; you'll decide on cook day

OR

- Scenario B
  - o Meet with the head chef and have a conversation where you share the following info:
    - You're having a party for 50 people
    - You'd like a mix of chicken, hot dogs, burgers and sides
    - Delivery must be included
    - Some of your friends are "foodies" with high expectations for flavor and presentation
    - You have a budget goal of $2,800

Which approach do you think will lead to a better experience for your party guests? If you chose "B", you are correct! Let's consider why.

In example "A", no conversation ever takes place about what your guests will actually experience. The request also assumes that YOU (vs the chef) know exactly what is required to feed your party guests. What is more likely? That YOU would know exactly how many ovens, how many cooks, how many spoons, how much time, etc. is required from your favorite restaurant kitchen to feed your 50 guests, or the chef who runs the restaurant for a living?

In example "A" because the actual food to be cooked is unknown until it's "go" time, how does the restaurant prepare properly? Do you imagine that all food is the same and that any random chef can complete your order? Of course not. As it turns out, A/V support follows those same rules.

In example "A" if your guests dining experience turns out to be meh… and you were expecting amazing, where does that responsibility lie? With the chef? With the dishwasher? Possibly with you?

(At this point, it's OK if you're hungry… grab a snack; I'll meet you back here in a few minutes.)

The above food "example B" may sound silly, but in practice, that is EXACTLY how A/V support is often procured by well-meaning clients and supplied by well-meaning vendors

Whether you are a 40 year meeting industry veteran or a part-time office admin tasked with organizing a meeting for the very first time, planning great meetings and events involves much more than just negotiating "dates and rates". Anytime you put a group of people together in the same place at the same time, you are creating, literally from nothing, something special, something unique, something amazing, something magical; you are creating a moment in time. That moment, will never exist again. What do you want that moment to say about your company? About you?

Quick Tip for Planners and Stakeholders: Do you want to capture your meeting on video to save it for later? (Handy for a training presentation to make the content available on demand via web.) Your costs could be substantially lower if that service is negotiated early in the conversation vs last minute as an "Oh crap!" ad-on.

When thinking about your meeting strategy, what should the audience feel "in the moment?" What do you want them to remember 30 days later? How are the meeting stake-holders measuring the meeting's success? How do we, working together from different sides of the isle, (meeting planner and A/V provider) get them there?

During meetings I see many companies say to their audience things like "YOU'RE THE BEST!" and "We are the LEADERS", and "Everything we do is STATE OF THE ART!" But the message is delivered with mediocrity as a result of bad choices made early in the process.

When an important or inspiring message is delivered with mediocrity, mediocrity then becomes the real message. Your employees are smart. And a modern audience's expectations are lofty; they experience great performances all the time. Do you really believe that you can "fool" a modern audience or get by with a minimal effort?

Those companies are, by their actions, saying to the audience "You're not worth the effort to get this right." "You don't' deserve a high-quality experience today." "We expect perfection from you as an employee, but you should be satisfied with mediocrity from your company and its leadership."

Your message is your brand, your image, your purpose, your EVERYTHING. The content that delivers and reinforces that message has a big job. It has to be relevant. It has to be vibrant. It has to be effective. It has to be on point. It has to be whatever it has to be to share your message, and achieve your outcome. And it probably needs some A/V support while it's being presented.

A table is a table, a chair is a chair, a microphone is.... irrelevant... without something to amplify.

From here forward, we are renaming "A/V" to "A/V support" which better describes its true role.

A/V equipment on its own does nothing. (Ok, so it does occasionally catch on fire...) It is a TOOL to deliver content to an audience. Stage lights? Their purpose is to illuminate a stage and the people on that stage so the presenter isn't in the dark and looks great on camera, in photos and in the moment to the live audience. Sound system? Its purpose is to deliver the words of the keynote and to the audience. Video screens and projectors? Their purpose is to deliver PowerPoint presentations, photo slide-shows, live camera feeds, produced videos, etc. to the audience.

So, why take the time, YOUR time, to make the case for A/V equipment being tools that support a larger purpose vs being an "actual thing" that stands on its own? Glad you asked!

Very often we'll receive a request that goes something like this:

Client "Hi! I'd like to rent a screen, a projector, and a wireless microphone."

Me: "Excellent! When would you like to pick them up?"

Client: "We also need someone to deliver them."

Me: "No problem at all. It sounds like you have someone there who will be operating the equipment?"

Client: "Can the person delivering the equipment plug in our laptop to the projector before they leave?"

Me: "We're glad to help! You asked for delivery at 4PM. So just to verify, the laptop with the presentation will also be there at 4PM?"

Readers with some experience, I can already see you cringing… as you know where this conversation is headed. The client is setting themselves up for failure by asking all the wrong questions and making any number of terrible assumptions.

Assumption 1) The laptop with the presentation will be there when the equipment is delivered.

Assumption 2) The laptop with the presentation will not be needed for anything else and can remain connected to the projector until the presentation is complete.

Assumption 3) The laptop is working correctly/configured correctly/is reliable.

Assumption 4) The PowerPoint is "show ready" meaning the presentation is in the same format as the screen and all the slides are correct, have working links to media, etc.

Assumption 5) The text size of the presentation and the physical size of the screens are matched to the room size so all guests can read the text on the screen.

Assumption 6) The wireless microphone will work correctly, will not squeak or squeal, and everyone will be able to hear the presentation clearly.

Assumption 7) All the equipment will work perfectly when the presentation starts, just like it did a few hours before when setting up.

Assumption 8) The electrical power/wall outlet will work perfectly during the presentation, just like it did during setup.

Assumption 9) No guests will ever trip on something or walk into something without paying attention and knock over a speaker or projector or screen or microphone and all the equipment will need to be reset.

We could do this all day…

Rather than trying to list the literally hundreds of ways a small presentation like this could fail, let's look at how we can help it succeed. A better conversation might go something like this:

Client *"Hi! I'm in charge of a new product training meeting for 50 people. We will be in a small ballroom at _____ hotel." I'm being told that there will be two presenters, a PowerPoint presentation and a Q&A session. What A/V support do I need for this?"*

Me: *"How is the room set up?" "Theater? Classroom? Rounds?"*

Client: *"Classroom"*

Me: *"Perfect! Do you know which ballroom?"*

Client: *"Yes, Blueberry Basket Breakout Rooms 1 & 2"*

Me: *"As this is a product training, would you like to video record the presentation so your team can use it as a resource in the future*

Client: *"Yes, that would be great!"*

Me: *"Let's talk about the presentation. What is the training aiming to accomplish? What will the PowerPoint look like?"*

Client: *"The training is for the product reps to learn how to sell the new product line. The PowerPoint will contain lots of detailed drawings that explain how the products work."*

Me: *"Great. That room has ceiling speakers so we can tie the microphone in to them and save you some money. But the room is kind of long and narrow so we suggest a slightly larger video screen so everyone at the back can see the presentation clearly." You and I will work together to make sure the PowerPoint presentation looks great on the screen we'll be using in that ballroom. It sounds like you need a wireless microphone, sound mixer, one-size-up video screen, video projector, laptop with PowerPoint remote and an operator to pull everything together."*

As you can see, this is a much higher quality conversation. Rather than the client opening the conversation believing they already know **how** to accomplish their goal and moving immediately into the "how much" phase, we spend a few minutes so that I can understand **what** the goals are. This enables me to add proprietary knowledge to the conversation (Room has ceiling speakers, we can use them and save money.) (Long and narrow room shape + PowerPoint with detailed drawings = slightly larger video screen required for all guests to see clearly.)

What should start becoming clear at this point is that a great A/V support provider is really a consultant first, supplier second. Because you've asked the right questions from chapter 1, you are speaking with a provider who is knowledgeable, experienced, and has certifications to help you feel comfortable that they are not "shooting from the hip" or offering suggestions which are not based on best practices.

Building on that foundation, a great A/V support provider has participated in hundreds if not thousands of meetings just like yours. That means they have watched hundreds if not thousands of hours of content, (which we know is what really matters), just like yours.

Your marketing department may be convinced that the video clip of the singing pumpkin will *kill* when the audience sees it… but a second opinion might be the secret sauce to landing on final content that actually does move the audience right to the place you want them.

A different question to ask if you are about to spend LOTS of MONEY on fancy content from a graphics or media company is WHY? Why are we (you the buyer) spending X amount of resources on fancy flying logos and Academy awards style imaging. Does it really support your meeting purpose? If yes, then awesome! It sounds like you're on the road to a meeting that will be a good use of company resources and will reward the investment of everyone's time to attend. Because you are asking the right questions and putting your priorities in the right order.

So, how do we (you and you're A/V support provider) DELIVER that content? What size video screens do you need in the actual room where the meeting is taking place? How powerful do the projectors need to be? More powerful than necessary spends your money but doesn't buy your audience anything. Less powerful than necessary and you're back to meh.

Quick tip: If you're a meeting or event stake-holder, the only outcome "meh" delivers with any consistency is water cooler chat that can be less than positive. If your ideas don't match up with your resources, consider other ideas that can be delivered with impact and excellence.

Visual content is potentially the biggest opportunity area to be impactful to an audience (rom meat and potatoes PowerPoint presentations to video mapping and 360 degree immersive experiences). Video content is also the most expensive. It is not uncommon for the video support to cost more than everything else combined. That does not mean your money is wasted! On the contrary, dollar for dollar, investing in visual content and the infrastructure to deliver it, can be the most effective use of your resources. But you and your A/V support provider MUST work together to determine what makes the most sense for you so you can make the right choices.

Just know that the road to great outcomes, outcomes that are impactful, moving and measurably effective, is rarely paved by considering A/V equipment and the content it will be supporting, in isolation. If you secure the equipment in one silo, and create the content in another, what are the chances that when they are combined on show site that the final result meets your expectations? There's a very real chance that everything will come together. Or not. Is the night before your big sales kickoff the best time to find out?

Sometimes we are asked to support a portion of an event but not everything. This is always an opportunity to observe what could have been done better. One interesting, real life example we see often in large general sessions is the audio system vs. the closing night entertainment. The client said yes to a large, powerful audio system that delivers excellent speech quality to every chair. But when the band or DJ shows up for the final night party, only then is it discovered that no loudspeakers point at the dance floor. Because of how those systems work, areas of no audio coverage are dramatically quieter than the areas with coverage. No sound; no party. At that point it becomes a scramble to cobble something together so the entertainment can "get through" the night. The client spends more money on an emergency solution than the right solution would have cost if the content of entertainment was included in the planning. The extra stress on everyone in that moment is free of charge… Here, where cooler heads prevail, we can all agree that is not a good example of owning your outcome.

Consider this basic truth: the most expensive screen and projector that money can buy may result in unreadable text at the back of the room if the PowerPoint uses text that is too small. Alternately, a much more modest screen and projector may work great in that same room if the PowerPoint text is sized correctly.

The OUTCOME (everyone in the audience being able to read the PowerPoint slide) depends first on the actual slides themselves, and second on the specific screen and projector. While this may sound self-evident, I see over and over and over… the look of disappointment on client's faces when the PowerPoint that looked great on the high definition big screen TV in their conference room, looks terrible on the screen and projector they ordered for their meeting. The same PowerPoint that the client brought with them an hour before the presentation and now they don't have time to rebuild.

A different way to think about the PowerPoint and screen dilemma is if you are sitting 10 feet away from a 60 inch TV in your conference room, think about how far away your guests will sit from the screen at your meeting, then just scale up. A 60 inch TV = about a 4.5 foot screen, so at 20 feet of distance you would need a 9 foot screen, at 40 feet of distance you would need a 18 foot screen, and at 80 feet of distance you would need a 36 foot screen for your guests to enjoy the same thing that you are viewing in your conference room. Now, take a look at your seating chart again. That 8 foot screen you are considering ordering, what will your guests actually see from 80 feet away?

I can't force a client to complete (or even begin!) the PowerPoint ahead of time, where it can be tested to work properly during prep and I can't force a client to buy the most expensive screen and projector available "just in case." But I can suggest to you that ordering A/V equipment, and building your content as two unrelated tasks, is flirting with failure and is NOT a great way to OWN YOUR OUTCOMES.

Another example I see all the time involves the playback of videos. These can be anything from a product demo to a "feel-good" reel. The client will mention during the consult that they would like a video to be played during the presentation. Not a problem, one video can often be accommodated with a regular Mac or PC laptop at minimal cost. But once onsite, that video becomes three videos, and each video needs to start at a specific moment during the presentation. *("When the CEO says 'watermelon' the slide show needs to end and the watermelon video should start immediately, etc.")*

Now we have a problem. Reliable, "on-cue" playback of multiple videos requires a more specialized tool. A Playback Pro system is one such tool. It's built for the job, is an industry standard and is used successfully every day around the world. It's also a bit more expensive than a regular laptop.

What happens next in the one video becomes three example, is usually some flavor of disappointment. Either the final presentation using the regular laptop is not to the expectations/vision of the client or the additional cost to bring in the right tool at the last minute becomes a source of stress for both the client and for the show team. The client demanding that the operator "JUST MAKE IT WORK!" when that client didn't order the correct tool, sets the show team up to fail, sets the meeting planner/event producer up to fail and sets the guests up for disappointment.

A great irony here is that while the cost for the meeting planner may be slightly higher to order the correct tool, the actual profit for the A/V provider may actually be lower when providing the more specialized system and operator for that system.

Quick Tip: For anyone involved with hiring an A/V provider, don't assume that you are being "upsold" more expensive equipment just to increase someone's holiday bonus. (That same A/V provider would LOVE to offer you the less expensive option, that is easier for their team to fulfill while also being more profitable! With integrity, the provider has a responsibility to propose the correct tool for the job, giving their client the choice of how to proceed.)

Let's go back in time and ask the question "How did that happen?" And more importantly, how do we prevent it? Most likely, it happened by considering in isolation the A/V equipment and the content that A/V equipment will support. How do we prevent a scenario like this from happening? Simple; ALWAYS start with the content.

In this case, the client incorrectly assumed that changing the scope of the presentation, would not have any impact on what was required to present said content.

If you are a camping type and tow a small trailer with your midsize car, then suddenly upgrade to a much larger and heavier trailer, would you expect to reliably and safely tow that much larger trailer with your mid-size sedan, just because the sedan has a trailer hitch? Of course not. You need the correct tool for the job. A/V support works the same way.

Providers don't expect their clients to understand or know all the nitty-gritty details of how things get accomplished, that is why the client is hiring an expert, but providers DO expect their clients to trust them and to not make blanket assumptions that can get everyone into trouble.

Quick Tip: For anyone involved with negotiating/hiring an A/V provider, and/or managing onsite: Because many A/V solutions are highly specialized, it may not be possible to change the scope (one video play back to three videos playback in this example) without changing out the equipment and possibly the operators of the equipment.

In the planning phase, with trust, clients and providers need to have a conversation about goals as well as what "might" also happen. A decision can be made at that time about whether it makes sense to purchase the "best" equipment as insurance or stick with "good" or "better" equipment at lower cost with the understanding that if the scope changes onsite, another conversation will need to take place. With trust, that second conversation can also be collaborative instead of combative. The client and provider need to again work together to make the best possible choices in that moment for the guests, while also respecting the wishes, vision and budget of the meeting or event stakeholders.

We know that in meetings and events things change all the time, it's the dynamic nature of show business. It's what makes the profession interesting and fun. But everyone shares responsibility to get an event or meeting across the finish line. The A/V provider has the responsibility of asking the right questions, delivering the right solutions, and being mindful of their client's resources. The client has the responsibility of asking their stakeholders the right questions, adequately understanding the scope of their meeting and critically, accepting the possibility that if the scope changes, then different tools might be required. It's the nature of the highly specialized solutions that are typical in A/V.

Also, if the scope changes at the last possible moment, (like in rehearsal!) then some compromise might be in order. It's not realistic to expect the A/V provider to move a mountain to procure the correct tool and the correct technician, at the last possible moment, and not adjust the final invoice unless it was their mistake. As a rule, if the provider makes a mistake or miscalculation about what is required to deliver the outcomes discussed in advanced, then the provider will make the adjustments in equipment and crew, along with their sincere apology! And if the provider did not ask their client the right questions in advance, shame on them! On the other hand, I have worked with (and fired) clients with expectations and demands that are simply not realistic. Clients who are dishonest or make bad choices, then yell "JUST MAKE IT WORK!" at the show team, create a negative, hostile, poisonous environment that I choose not to participate in.

Please don't be one of those clients! Great A/V providers want you to be happy, want you to not stress, want you to feel like you received more than you paid for and want to partner with you for years and years. AND, if your provider doesn't make you feel happy, valued, unstressed, and like you always receive great value; switch! There are LOTS of providers in every city who would welcome the opportunity to earn your business. It's a two-way street!

ACTION STEPS you can use RIGHT NOW

(Applies to anyone involved with vetting and hiring an A/V provider, and needing special accommodations from said provider)

- *Understand the scope of the content that will be presented before you procure the A/V equipment that will present it*
- *Don't make assumptions that if the scope of your needs changes, the A/V equipment you have will automatically support those changes*

- *Don't expect that because a PowerPoint looked great on the TV in your conference room, it will look great on any random screen and projector*
- *Understand that non-professionally produced content, (e.g. many YouTube videos, non color-corrected slide shows, etc.) that looks ok'ish to decent on your conference room TV may look terrible on the big screen at your meeting*
- *Don't assume everything will just "come together" onsite*

Chapter 4

Ego

This chapter is for industry veterans who have "been around the block" a time or two, and work extra hard to make sure everybody around them knows how awesome they are.

Let's talk about ego. This is a perfect opportunity to take a good, long, honest look at your ego, and how you interact with others. I've personally completed several "ego audits" and each time, made changes to my own behavior, particularly, how I speak to (or at) others.

Are you an experienced meeting planner/event industry veteran/producer, etc. and after reading the last chapter your response, (said with the deprecating snicker of someone who is highly experienced, and VERY IMPORTANT), is *"PSHAWWW! I don't have time for this…l I know exactly what I need…, just give me the PRICE so I can move on to my next task…* " If that sounds like you, then consider conducting an ego audit on yourself. What if your words, your tone, and maybe your own perception is that you are the smartest person in the room… what if your inflated opinion of yourself is actually cheating your clients and their audiences of the best possible experiences and best cost/value for their outcomes?

Are you a big-enough person to consider that? And to have this grown-up conversation?

Great leaders are willing to take a step back and ask themselves and others, how they can improve, what they need to do next to keep growing, and how to be something better tomorrow then they are today. Great leaders also recognize that they need the help of others to be successful.

Steve Jobs famously said *"It doesn't make sense to hire smart people and tell them what to do; we hire smart people so they can tell us what to do."*

If you are a meeting planner, or event producer, when securing providers, (including A/V) do you hire smart people, then tell them what to do? If yes, why? Do you consider yourself the smartest person in the room?

Maybe you legitimately are the smartest person in the room regarding your provider's area of expertise, but what does that say about your choice of providers and about your standards?

As it relates to A/V, if you've hired a great provider, that provider will be more knowledgeable about their craft than you. Your value in the conversation is your creative ability and your vision. You win by doing whatever it takes to communicate with perfect clarity, your vision to the provider, until you are convinced they "get it." Then you must step out of the way and let them tell you how your vision comes to life and how it gets implemented. This is how Steve Jobs worked. Do you think you're smarter than Steve Jobs?

YES, I'm being provocative. And I will continue to poke you in the nose until you raise your hand and acknowledge that you're listening.

If, in your heart of hearts, some of the bad behaviors mentioned here sound like you, then I challenge you to get out of your own head and into the head of your newest, least experienced team member. Or into the head of your least experienced, most nervous client; the one that fears they will lose their job if something goes wrong during the meeting you're working on with them. Try and imagine what they see, hear and feel. Are YOU the impression of this great industry they will remember? Is what they see, hear, experience and feel interacting with you, is that the positive and good energy you want to project out into the universe? Or are you projecting something else?

I would bet that when you started in this industry, it was with great excitement, a sense of idealism, and you were energized by the child-like wonder of what was possible. You dreamed of making a difference for your guests, of executing complex plans, and creating beauty and once-in-a-lifetime moments. How would that junior version of you enjoy dealing with the current you? Would it want to emulate the current you or vow to be nothing like you?

That's how I begin my own personal ego audits. They're tough to complete. It's difficult to look in the mirror and recognize that sometimes, I've been a jerk and treated people badly. Once the audit is complete, and I've identified bad behaviors, forgiven myself, and moved forward, it seems that the world is a slightly better place, both for me and for everyone that I interact with.

Only you know the questions to ask yourself in an ego audit. Really, just try it. If after going through the exercise you don't find any benefit at all, then you can toilet paper my house next Halloween… but what if the audit works? Think of how you change the mood, the day, and the experience of everyone around you, of everyone that interacts with you. There's more that's really good from this self-exploration, but I'll let you discover that for yourself.

Quick Tip. If you are a meeting planner or event producer and need a quote quickly and working with a challenging budget, or require special accommodations from the A/V vendor for any reason, etc. consider being upfront and truthful. And respectful. And Nice. Drop the ego. (Don't make yourself sound like the "DO YOU KNOW WHO I AM???" person) As a provider, I have a LOT of latitude to solve your problems with solutions you might not know exist and at prices much more flexible than you might expect. How tall of a mountain do you honestly think I will want to move for you if you're communicating using threats, being disrespectful/over-important, or are just highly unpleasant to be around. It's your choice either way, but at least consider taking a step back and working collaboratively with your A/V support provider. You might be pleasantly surprised!

The moral of the story here is don't be a jerk. Qualify your provider appropriately, be truthful about your goals, then let them help you look and be successful.

ACTION STEPS you can use RIGHT NOW:

(Applies in particular to highly experienced meeting and event professionals, but valid for everyone)

- *Don't be a jerk*
- *Don't always assume you know everything*
- *Don't be denigrating, disrespectful, ungrateful, or over-important*
- *Don't forget that lots of people contributed in some way over the years to your success*
- *Don't be afraid to be humble and grateful, it actually can feel really good*

Chapter 5

Success Depends on the Team, NOT the Hardware

Let's say you are a meeting planner or event producer and have been asked to create and present a new concept to your best client, and the presentation is in 10 days. If the presentation goes well, it's a big leap forward for you professionally. If the presentation goes poorly, then you'll probably lose your job. (You know, just like every meeting or event!)

Not being a PowerPoint expert, or digital graphics and imaging expert, you ask for some resources and the "powers that be" say yes. So you rent a super-powerful computer, with the latest software, a PowerPoint remote control to rehearse with, a fancy large screen monitor, you even secure a "don't disturb" room with perfect lighting for the ideal creative and working environment. You make sure there are lots of snacks and coffee, and finally, you tell the computer rental place to "just send someone" to translate your vision and ideas to digital and help you create the actual PowerPoint presentation.

Of course, you wouldn't blindly accept someone randomly chosen by the computer place; someone with the power to make or break your job or career based on their performance with your project. And with integrity, the computer rental place wouldn't "just send someone" to do a job with such high stakes, without asking some important questions in advance.

First, you need the person who creates the presentation to "speak the same language" creatively, as you, plus be skilled in digital with building PowerPoint presentations like the one you need to build. Plus, the person must be dependable, understand how you work, understand how to work with you, understand "what you mean" vs what you ask, be effective working with your internal team, understand the stakes attached to the project, work with excellence inside your deadline, etc. You need to get this campaign right to score the win. Or you lose your job.

That above example looks only at building a PowerPoint presentation in a non-show environment. What about executing all the technical elements, on cue, with "one shot" only, for an entire meeting or session or performance? If you are hiring an A/V provider to support your meeting or event, what do you know about their team? What do you know about the person or people YOU are depending on for your success? Are you assuming that they are of a certain skill level and experience? Do you trust without verifying?

Confronted with these questions, it's normal for meeting planners and event producers to suggest that it's the provider's job to qualify, vet, hire, train and manage their team. And that sentiment is 100% correct.

But what about in practice? What about for YOUR meeting or event?

Does every chef, every auto technician, every painter, everyone you've ever hired, do they meet or exceed your expectations the first time? What about the second time? When did you choose to move on to someone else?

With meetings there are no do-overs. There is no "take-back" of your car or sending lunch back to the kitchen or hiring a different painter to fix the crooked lines or wrong colors of the first painter.

The deadline is the deadline. And your reputation hangs in the balance. How much of your success are you willing to leave to chance? How much are you willing to trust blindly that the provider has perfectly understood your needs and requirements? Or that the provider has the exact team you need, just sitting around ready to be plugged into your event? Or that the provider has accurately (meaning honestly) represented their talents and abilities, and, is looking out for you and your success first, and his profit last?

YOU as the customer have not only the right, but the responsibility to ask about your show team. It is your job to meet them and speak with them as part of your buying process. And it's your job to look at their resumes, understand their experience, and decide if you are comfortable working with them. Is this the team you are ready to stake your reputation on? If this sounds like a job interview, then yes, you are correct. If during the course of meeting with (i.e. interviewing) your show team, you get a bad feeling, isn't that a better scenario than getting that same bad feeling 10 minutes before opening the doors while the CEO is yelling at you because something has gone wrong?

Meet with and approve your show team in advance. This is an important step to OWNING YOUR OUTCOMES.

Quick Tip: The best quality team using the worst quality equipment (that functions) will generally deliver a better overall outcome than the best quality equipment operated by the lowest quality technicians.

There, I said it.

This is not something that A/V providers will tell you during a sales presentation (they want you to rent their fancy new equipment) but it is something they say to each other over adult beverages.

Why is that? Ask yourself, what would a prospect find more interesting?

"On your event we would like to suggest the latest new video projectors. They use laser beams!"

(Then cue the demo or talking points.)

Or

"For your event, we strongly recommend putting _____ on your show team. He's expensive... you'll have to give up a few bells and whistles but he gets every client across the finish line every time, especially with complicated meetings like yours.."

Quite simply, it's a tough sell to a client or prospect. The fancy new projector is tangible, the talent level of an invisible technician is intangible. Plus, in many regions, the best talent isn't even available locally, which means more cost to you after flying them in from somewhere else, plus lodging, etc.

Think back to the intro of this book. The only reason that event actually happened was because of the people behind the curtain. NOTHING mattered in those moments leading up to "doors" other than the skill and resolve of that show team to get the equipment "patched up" and to help the client deliver the amazing experience those 3000 people had been anticipating all year.

As a meeting planner or event producer, it may be tempting to focus on décor, entertainment, food and beverage; all the things you can see and touch, but ask yourself "If the CEO's presentation (or whatever is important at your meeting) failed completely, what would be the impact on this event or meeting?" If it doesn't matter, then you have your answer; and should spend your money somewhere else where it do the most good.

Like a highly-efficient, impartial jury, the "What if it fails?" question is a time-tested way of getting to the truth. It is an effective way to draw lines between needs, wants, and resources. For instance, I may *want* to drive a vintage hot-rod, but what I *need* is a reliable car that will get me to work every day in 100+ degree Florida heat.

I have worked with clients who prefer to spend more of their meeting budget on snacks than on A/V support. I respect and support that as a thoughtful choice. But, those clients and I work together to make good decisions about what's important, and how we can balance their needs against their wants. A client may want 400 feet of sparkling drape in their meeting room, but they need everyone to actually see the PowerPoint and hear the presenter.

Maybe spending more budget on snacks is the right choice for some meetings. BUT, inside the pages of this book we can be honest with each other. Did you demand the "good" A/V package when the supplier strongly recommended the "better" or "best" one? Do you think the supplier recommended the better packages only to price-gouge or are you willing to consider that maybe the better packages are what's actually required to deliver what you are asking for? These are questions only you can answer but they are questions that you must ask.

If your budget places more importance on snacks (or table centerpieces or whatever) than on A/V support, who bears the responsibility if the microphone doesn't work when the CEO walks on stage after you said "no" to the solution the provider recommended? Where does "at the end of the day" responsibility fall if the wrong video clip is played at the tear-jerking moment of your fundraiser? Or someone on the tech team makes an inappropriate comment that offends one of your C-suite executives? Or a critical piece of equipment starts to catch fire? Sure, you can have a conversation with the provider after the fact about a refund or some other consideration, but by that point your meeting has failed.

Look in the mirror and be honest with yourself about the choices you make. If something meets the standard of "if it fails, that would be catastrophic" then it's your responsibility to ensure 'that something" doesn't fail. This is an important step to OWNING YOUR OUTCOMES.

A colleague shared with me the story of attending a particular networking event. He had been looking forward to this event and drove some distance to attend. His "hit list" included several high-value prospects along with a number of colleagues whom he always enjoyed reconnecting with.

For ambiance and to create some "vibe" the event featured a talented live musician who played the piano soulfully and sang with passion. This should have been the perfect addition to a great event; the frosting on the cake if you will, except that the music as delivered by the A/V provider, was SOOOO LOOOUDDD, actual networking was effectively impossible.

How did this happen? Let's assume the worst, and imagine the meeting planner or event producer in charge of the event was for whatever reason unable to be there and provide managing guidance. And the meeting planner chose to not include a technical manager in the A/V package. The "boots on the ground" equipment operator should know, without a doubt, how to set an appropriate volume level for a networking function.

But really, we are talking about a decision of "taste" and not everyone shares the same ability to make good decisions of taste. Maybe that operator, a "get it done" working type, has never attended a networking event as a guest, and therefore has no frame of reference for what the perfect networking event look, feels, and sounds like. Thinking he is doing a good job, the operator doesn't realize that he is ruining the event.

Sometimes, I observe operators deeply enjoying the entertainment they are supporting, and as a result, make decisions that are not in the best interest of the actual event audience. The operator treats the event like their own personal mini-concert, and as a result, the guests suffer. The outcome in this case has nothing to do with the quality or quantity of equipment provided, or how much money was spent on A/V. EVERYTHING in those scenarios comes down to choices made by the equipment operator.

As the client, it is your right (and responsibility) to provide sufficient guidance to your A/V show team so they can deliver your outcomes as you expect them. But how often have you worked with A/V folks who just didn't "get it"? You tell them one thing but they continue to do it their way? Or is the real problem that you never discussed your desired outcome in advance and the paid-by-the-hour subcontracted operator who has never attended a networking event (but has attended lots of concerts) did the best they could until you told them to "**TURN IT DOWN!!**" in an angry tone?

I promise, it doesn't have to be this way. It may seem rudimentary and obvious to you (It's your event!) what outcomes the A/V show team is supporting, but many of those good (and some not so good) people come from different worlds than you. And if you wait until the last minute to book a provider, their best people were probably assigned to other meetings or events many months prior.

If you've met with and approved your show team in advance, scenarios like the one my colleague experienced are all but eliminated. Sure, anyone can have a bad day, but because you've requested technicians who are experienced and skilled in events like yours, and because you've discussed in advance your outcomes and expectations, and because you feel comfortable that your show team understands exactly what you are trying to accomplish, you will have the luxury of actually enjoying the event, in a stress-free environment, the same as your guests.

If you are the person responsible for procuring A/V support for a networking event like the one my colleague attended, we all know it is highly unlikely that anyone will approach you after the event and thank you for choosing an A/V provider with the right equipment and operators, that helped set the perfect vibe, which then put everyone in a great mood, and enabled them to convert a prospect to a client, which made it possible for their kids to go to college. Likely, no one will say that to you, because you know that great A/V support is invisible. But they ABSOLUTELY will remember for months, even year's later, if the event (and their future business possibilities) failed. And it's possible someone WILL approach you personally about how your event was a failure. That will be your black eye in the eyes of others.

ACTION STEPS you can use RIGHT NOW:

(Applies to anyone vetting and/or hiring an A/V provider)

- *Interview your show team (Yes, this requires a small investment of your time)*
- *Don't "settle" for a team you're not comfortable with*
- *Make sure your approved team is named on the contract (vs a generic position)*
- *NEVER assume a generic show team is qualified, competent, experienced, knows "what you mean" or will work to your standards*

Chapter 6

Agree to Standards

Building on the previous example, let's say you as the meeting planner or event producer, against your provider's recommendation, decide to move forward with the "good" A/V package and the "best" snacks package for your next important function. During the presentation, the microphone squeaks and squeals, distracting from if not ruining the presentation.

My question to you is a simple one: What does your contract say?

This idea is so obvious it probably sounds insulting, but for all of us as an industry to truly make progress, it's the next step. Along with contractual "dates and rates" did you ever have a conversation with the provider about performance standards? If yes, did you define those standards and put them in writing in your agreement?

Over and over, I see contracts that are painfully detailed about dates, rates, parts, pieces, even listing exact quantities of nuts, bolts, and rolls of tape. But these same agreements say NOTHING about performance standards. Zero. Nada. Zilch. It's as if performance standards aren't "even a thing" until the actual meeting or event is taking place.

What is the yardstick that you will use to measure your provider's performance once the meeting or event is complete? That's what you should be talking about in advance and specifying on your contract.

If you are working with an A/V provider to help deliver a presenter's words to your audience, likely you will have spoken about microphones, loudspeakers, loudspeaker stands and decorative skirts, sound mixers, audio technicians, "load-in" schedules, overtime rates, etc.

But what are you actually buying? What did the provider actually sell you? Everything listed above are merely tools. What about the outcome? Isn't the outcome what you're actually buying?

In truth, you're buying "reinforcement of the presenter's voice" so that everyone can hear the presentation clearly and without distractions. Even though the hardware, and tools, and show team are "tangible" and easy to list on a quote or invoice, what you are actually buying is the outcome of your audience hearing the presentation.

Do you see how this is now a very different conversation?

Once you've defined what you're actually buying, how do you then define and measure "good" vs "great" vs "bad"?

When prospects ask me about sound reinforcement for the spoken word of presenters, I offer an easy to understand (and measure) standard. **"Natural sounding, perfectly intelligible dialog at every seat, with no "feedback" and no missed cues."**

This clearly stated idea is incredibly powerful because it makes the conversation about "what" (the outcome and performance standard) vs "how" (four loudspeakers, two microphones, one technician, plus delivery, etc.)

And, because the standard is so easy to measure, if its defined and I don't deliver, the client has grounds to not pay. Is the presenter, as delivered through the sound system, natural sounding? Is their voice perfectly intelligible? Is that outcome happening at every seat? Is the microphone "feeding back" (those annoying squeaks, chirps, and squeals) or is the sound clear and free of those annoyances? Did the microphone smoothly turn on when the presenter walked up to it or was the presenter greeted by a microphone that was turned off then abruptly turned on while the presenter was banging it with their hand asking *"Is this on? Is this on? Can you hear me?"*

Meeting this standard actually requires sophisticated equipment and advanced operator skills. Most meeting locations have terrible acoustics and getting a natural sound in them can be quite the wrestling match. Getting sound is easy, getting **NATURAL** sound, much more difficult. (Many providers fail right here at this first step!) Next, intelligible sound is not always difficult, but perfectly intelligible sound that is also natural? This can be very difficult and often requires extremely high quality equipment and advanced techniques to make the equipment and room work together. Next, delivering the natural sounding, perfectly intelligible sound to EVERY SEAT, requires the correct number of loudspeakers (too few or too many can make meeting this standard impossible) plus advanced operator knowledge to make everything come together. The standards of no "feedback" and no missed cues fall directly on the skill and care of the operator.

So, to deliver on this standard:

- **Natural Sounding** - 80% result of highly skilled operator, 20% top quality equipment
- **Perfectly intelligible** - 80% result of highly skilled operator, 20% top quality equipment
- **Every seat** - 50% result of highly skilled operator 50% correct type/amount of equipment
- **No feedback** - 50% result of highly skilled operator 50% correct type/amount of equipment
- **No missed cues** - 100% result of highly skilled operator

Focusing the conversation with your provider on "what" you need delivered vs "how" it will be delivered gives everyone the information required to make better decisions, both in the buying and planning phases. And, if after you've done everything right and the provider is falling short somewhere, you can have a much more focused conversation with them. If during rehearsal the sound from the presenter is "muddy" or "tinny" or can't be heard clearly in the back rows of seating, you can then point to the agreed upon standard and demand they meet the standard and deliver what they promised. You can say something like *"I'm paying you for natural sounding, perfectly intelligible sound at every seat. (As you hold the contract in front of them.) You have 90 minutes to fix this."*

Because of what is actually involved to deliver a standard like "natural sounding, perfectly intelligible dialog at every seat, with no feedback and no missed cues" it is simply not realistic to assume that is the standard your provider will deliver (just because you think they should) if that was not discussed in advance.

It's very likely that if you were to have a conversation about this standard onsite with your provider, say during setup or rehearsal, your provider might tell you that they would need to bring out different equipment and/or a different show team to make it possible.

Wouldn't you rather have that conversation in your planning phase vs during rehearsal while the CEO is onstage?

A recent inquiry came in that went something like: "I need a quote for two screens, two projectors, four wireless microphones and a laptop with Microsoft Office, and delivery." That inquiry was followed up with a conversation focused on outcomes and expectations, not dates and rates. Time will tell if that prospect becomes a client, or feels a different provider is a better fit, but either way, that meeting planner is now looking through a different lens at the role of A/V support and at her own role in the outcome of that meeting.

If we go back to the *"I'd like to rent a screen, a projector, and a wireless microphone."* example in chapter 3, but now think in terms of outcomes and performance standards, we must ask ourselves this: how does an A/V provider, (even one with the best abilities and intentions) deliver a great outcome at a high standard to that example meeting's audience? The answer is they cannot. The example A/V buyer is relying on chance and luck. The provider is relying on past experience to determine what is most likely in that scenario, and will absolutely need to put some contingencies in place to get through the meeting. What if they don't guess correctly? Or are unwilling to "throw in for free" the extra equipment that is actually needed? Everyone is positioned to fail. The audience is robbed of the meetings true potential and ROI.

If that example A/V buyer is dissatisfied with the outcome during the meeting, do you think it's reasonable for them to be upset with the provider, (assuming the actual equipment is functioning and the contracted standards are met) when outcomes or performance standards were never discussed? Stress for everyone in those moments can be off the charts. The meeting planner and A/V provider will both go home at the end of their day, continuing to believe that they are foes, not partners.

To stop the madness, we must communicate with each other, but that requires speaking the same language.

As the buyer, there is no reason for you to stress or worry over not having extensive (or any!) technical knowledge or knowing everything about the equipment. For their part, the A/V provider likely knows little about your creative process or how you interact expertly with your clients or the nuances that set you apart from your colleagues. So, what then, is a common language that everyone can speak?

Outcomes, and standards, and costs. That is the common ground from which everything grows.

As a veteran A/V practitioner, if it was my money and my meeting, and working with a provider I trusted, the request would go something like this:

Me: *"Mr. Provider, I'm looking for some help with a meeting and was wondering if you're able to prepare a quote by 3PM today?"*

Provider: *"We can have it to you by 4PM, would that work?"*

Me: *"Yes I can make that work. Here's what we know right now. One day meeting for 50 senior execs in a small ballroom (less than 100' each direction), set classroom style. Set up in the morning, run-thru after lunch, then actual meeting mid-afternoon. Keynote presenter, with Q&A. It's a pharma company so PowerPoint is likely to be technical, one bigger screen is probably better than two smaller ones and the image must be very clear! Two Windows laptops with PowerPoint (one as spare) with high-powered remotes. Sound system must deliver natural sounding, perfectly intelligible dialog to every seat with no feedback and no missed cues. (Dialog only, no music or sound effects playback) Let's start with two wireless and 6 wired microphones. No lighting for now. Client likely to be "high-maintenance" so show team must be A+ and easy to work with. PowerPoint operator only, not editor. We'll need to set up a 30 minute meet and greet between my client and your show team before final approval. Client is looking to spend between $10,000 and $15,000. Call me with any questions, thanks!"*

This inquiry tactically includes and omits specific pieces of information.

Includes: (enough info for the provider to estimate a real quote)

- General scope
    - Meeting Description (SVP meeting)
    - Meeting location (small hotel ballroom)
    - Room setup (classroom)
- General Requirements
    - PowerPoint presentation
    - Keynote speech
    - Q&A session
- General Schedule (one day, load in, rehearsal, the presentation)
- General performance expectations
    - Attendees are senior execs (expecting high level of fit and finish)
    - Video playback will be a technical presentation and must be very clear
    - Audio must be clear and natural with perfect coverage and no feedback
    - Show team must be skilled and easy to work with
- General Budget Expectations
    - Client would like to spend between $10,000 and $15,000

The inquiry **does NOT include my interpretation of how I believe the provider should do their job**. The inquiry does not include specific quantities, makes and models of microphones, loudspeakers, projectors, etc. Nor does it dictate how many technicians should be there. Or what type of vehicle is used for delivery and any number of other, non-helpful bits of information that inhibit the provider from being able to do what they do best and bring their particular brand of excellence to my meeting.

ACTION STEPS you can use RIGHT NOW:

(Applies to anyone vetting and/or hiring an A/V provider)

- *Do not tell your A/V provider how you believe they should do their job*
  - *(A/V providers are people too… they get that same "special" feeling you do when somebody tells you how to do your job!)*
- *DO tell your provider exactly what performance standards you require, and have them write those standards into your contract*
- *You deserve to work with an A/V provider that is competent and that you can trust. (There are more than 11,000 A/V companies in the US alone. You are never 'stuck' with a particular provider!)*

Chapter 7

The RFP

We know that to OWN YOUR OUTCOMES

1) A/V support is a practiced discipline delivered as a service
2) Perfectly executed A/V support is invisible
3) It's all about the content
4) Nobody wins when egos are in charge
5) Success depends on the team, not the hardware
6) Buyer and provider must agree on performance standards

And yet...

A very common method of procuring A/V support is via R.F.P. (request for proposal) or R.F.Q. (request for quote) These documents are essentially a list of pieces and parts, and a deadline for a quote.

RFPs violate nearly every rule for achieving great outcomes.

Often, R.F.Ps/R.F.Q.s for A/V support are very detailed regarding specific quantities and brands of equipment, and "body counts" to operate that equipment. What isn't covered in the document is most of what actually matters towards achieving the final outcome.

What is the meeting's purpose?   ~~crickets~~

What are the meeting's goals?   ~~crickets~~

How will the meeting's success be measured? ~~crickets~~

What are the client's expectations of fit and finish? ~~crickets~~

What about the content? ~~crickets~~

RFP's take away, with surgical precision, every provider's ability to apply their unique solutions to your specific wants and needs. RFP's are a highly effective way to make sure meeting guests see and experience the same thing over and over, year after year. They are engineered mediocrity.

For an A/V provider, RFP's are the final step in executing someone else's solution. If you're a provider and responding to an RFP, all the thinking, dreaming, and planning has been done. The buyer is simply looking for the lowest priced provider to execute the plan. Even if that plan is broken or terrible.

This is an article I wrote in 2015 when starting to grapple with the problem of RFP's. It's all I'm going to say about RFP's before we move on.

Speaking amongst colleagues, one of the topics that consistently elicits moans groans, or ...worse, is the RFP. It is my experience that most RFP's are poorly written, dishonest/misleading, or just plain wrong. In our office, we joke that RFPs are **Requests For Pantera.** When the iconic band's unmistakable sound of 1980s hair rock suddenly explodes from an account rep's desk, the entire office instantly knows what just happened; someone's been punished with being assigned an RFP.

As an audiovisual buyer, does your company still send out RFP's? As an audiovisual provider, does your company respond to RFP's? If yes, do you have a (secret) strategy to overcome their limitations and actually deliver a good outcome?

In the event business, RFP's are commonplace. And wrong. Let's look at some of the reasons why.

1) They Do Not Reference Outcome. Virtually every audiovisual RFP we receive includes a list of pieces and parts, (sometimes outdated or poor quality) often from events gone by, with no mention of the three REAL factors that actually determine cost.

A) Desired outcome with standards and benchmarks. Example RFP request: Stage Lighting for a keynote speaker, with list of pieces and parts used the previous year. The unwritten client expectation: perfectly even lighting with no shadows that simultaneously looks great on video in addition to the live audience along with extensive show cues that will be cobbled together by the client at the last minute during the wee hours the night before the 7AM show start.

Expectations and standards are rarely mentioned as they are likely to drive up cost if all parties are being honest. Additionally, it is often outside the expertise of the parties writing the RFP to realistically distinguish needs from wants or to understand the boundaries between overkill and inadequate.

B) Fit and finish (quality) expectations of the party writing the RFP and the team evaluating vendor submissions. Buyer expectations can include both outcome (for the guests) and overall buying experience (for the purchaser).

- Is the buyer submitting the RFP to vendors, a perfectionist that requires everything to look "perfect" or is low price more important?
- Does the buyer submitting the RFP to vendors, expect/require/prefer the "latest and greatest" technology or a proven solution at lower cost?
- Does the buyer submitting the RFP to vendors, require technical management and crew to be drug tested/background checked or is lower cost labor more important?

- Does the buyer submitting the RFP to vendors, require technicians who are certified in heavy equipment operation and rigging, or simply "hope" a less expensive non-certified crew knows what they are doing and will work safely?

C) Schedule/logistics can wildly affect the final cost and is rarely addressed in enough detail to be helpful in most RFP's.

- **Suppliers "game" the RFP** to submit it with the lowest possible price, knowing that they will make up the difference between the bid $ and the "real" $ with additional billing after winning the job. This is dishonest, and unethical, yet I'm told "everybody does it" for fear of losing the job if the RFP is answered honestly.
- **They are often a "rinse and repeat" or bottom-up approach** that cheats the guest by not exploring what's new, what's possible and what could be done better than last year. This can be due to a lack of specific knowledge of what is being purchased. Plus, sometimes it's possible for the buyer to spend less money while achieving a better outcome by taking a fresh and holistic look at the job which is not possible with RFPs. (Real solutions require a face-to-face to discuss outcome and expectations before presenting real solutions.)
- **They withhold or don't mention critical data** that will impact both outcome and cost.
    1. e.g. Last years' event was a disaster, yet the RFP includes the previous "solution" that didn't work.
    2. e.g. Last years' event went WAY over budget (because the RFP was submitted dishonestly) yet the same RFP with limited or wrong information is submitted a second year.
    3. The RFP lists the "on paper" solution from last year's supplier but the supplier actually included additional hardware and labor at no charge, (or submitted a second, unmentioned invoice after the event was completed) therefore, meeting the RFP will result in a lower quality outcome than expected.
- **RFP's commoditize the guest experience**.

1. If the outcome requires input and decisions from experts to provide the solution, it is not a commodity.
2. If the RFP is asking about apples, but oranges would serve the guests better, why are we talking about apples?

The RFP is an outdated, ineffective, often dishonest and mostly broken reminder of how NOT to do business. Meet JOE. Instead of sending an audiovisual RFP to your suppliers, request a *Job Outcome Estimate*. Instead of telling the supplier how YOU think they should do their job, (i.e. RFP for 6 stage lights, 2 screens, 2 projectors, 2 loudspeakers and a microphone) tell the supplier what you want to accomplish, i.e. lighting, video and sound for a live keynote with PowerPoint for a group of 300, classroom style. The best suppliers will then ask questions that help determine not only what is necessary to achieve the outcome, but *most importantly, determine what can sabotage the outcome* then include the solution in the rfp. (i.e. discovering the room is very "echoey" **and** has lots of ambient light from large windows that cannot be covered **and** all equipment must be hand carried up and down stairs **and** the event must be struck in one hour to accommodate another event immediately following, etc.)

A generic or typical RFP would most likely not address the four "gotchas" mentioned above, all of which have the potential to negatively impact everyone from client to guest to venue if discovered onsite.

ACTION STEPS you can use RIGHT NOW:

(Applies to anyone using an RFP for vetting and/or hiring an A/V provider)

- *STOP procuring A/V support via RFPs! Have a genuine conversation with great providers. Let them tell you how they will achieve your objectives, work to your standards and exceed your expectations.*

Chapter 8

About the Money

For many buyers, everything comes down to the money, and for EVERY buyer the conversation should be at least partially about the

money.

As a meeting planner or event producer, you have a responsibility to the event guests and to your stakeholders to make the best possible decisions with their resources.

Let's say we're trying to get up a dangerous hill and $10 guarantees a safe trip, and $9 gets you dropped off half way and it's up to you to climb the rest of the way, and survive… Is $9 a good value? Are you feeling lucky today? If your budget (real or pretend) is less than what's reasonably required to fulfill your requirements, what are you actually giving up to spend less?

All of us have fears when making important purchases and all of us want to get a great deal. That desire is only human! Maybe you've already asked for A/V quotes for a particular meeting or event but the prices are all over the place, sometimes varying by 200% - 300% or more. How is that possible?

How do we reconcile everything we now know with our innate desire to get a great deal? It is ABSOLUTELY possible for everyone to win when negotiating with an A/V provider where the guests win, the provider wins and you win. So how do we get there?

Achieving a win-win-win is easy if you follow this recipe:

Introducing U.C.B.MARK'N

1) Understand what problems you are trying to solve.
2) Communicate with your provider in a common language that everyone understands.
3) Be clear and honest about your expectations.
4) Make the provider prove their capabilities
5) Allow the provider to devise the solution.
6) Require the provider to document specific performance standards.
7) Know your team.
8) Never assume anything.

So much of the bad reputation the A/V industry has rightly earned is a result of both buyers and providers not following the simple recipe above. Eight easy steps.

Because the A/V industry has grown up organically, and because it is a practiced discipline delivered as a service, but quoted and negotiated as a product transaction, most people are speaking different languages all the time. And when nobody is speaking the same language, fears and assumptions can take over, and that's pretty much how the industry arrived at the place it is today; misunderstood, distrusted, known to be a weak link, and something to "deal with".

It is IMPOSSIBLE to compare quotes from one provider to another in any sort of meaningful way without a tight grip on U-C-B-MARK'N.

Stated a different way, without these eight steps, your outcome will essentially be left to chance. You are leaving YOUR OUTCOME in the hands of your provider and lady luck.

If you find yourself comparing quotes or estimates, and some estimates seem unusually low, ask yourself, why? What enables that provider to "beat" the other providers on price? If you were shopping for a brand-new car and one particular car dealer offers the same new model for half the price of anything else; wouldn't you be suspicious? Wouldn't you wonder "How can they do that?" The truth is, they can't. And neither can an A/V provider.

To begin answering the question "How can they do that?" let's peek behind the curtain into how the A/V industry functions.

There are three broad market sizes for A/V companies; small/local, medium/regional, and large/national-international. This is what they look like under the hood:

Small: 1 – 10 employees, one or two owners, maybe family owned.

What's great about a small company:

- Easy access to staff and owner/manger
- Willing to work harder for promise of future business
- Easy to "beat up" regarding their price

What's not so great about a small company:

- May not have the skills to fulfill their promises
- May not have the resources to meet your needs
- May not be financially stable or still in business in 6 months

Medium: 10 - 100 employees, might be owned by single person, partner group or equity funded

What's great about a medium company:

- Sweet spot for pricing, team strength, and financial stability
- Sufficient resources and talent to meet most needs
- Typically up to date with latest technology

What's not so great about a medium company

- Access may be more difficult
- May be overextended vs their capacity at certain times of the year
- May be "living on their laurels" from a previous time or owner

Large: up to thousands of employees, typically owned by private equity

What's great about large company:

- Extensive resources
- Unlimited capacity
- They've recently done hundreds of meetings or events just like yours

What's not so great about a large company

- Access to top talent may be very difficult
- May not be possible to choose your show team
- Quality can vary greatly from location to location

Here's how A/V providers keep their costs down

1) "Freelance" labor
   i. 1099 (non taxed) payment to show team and crew
   ii. Often no individual workers comp insurance or liability insurance

   iii. They are provided no benefits at all
   iv. Your show may be the first time they are working with your provider
   v. May be in violation of fair labor standards or federal tax laws

2) "Labor of Love" mentality of owner or management
   i. "Love" what they do
   ii. Willing to work long hours for little or no pay
   iii. Willing to work for little or no company profit
   iv. Willing to work inexpensively "this year" in the hopes of something better "next year"

3) Old/outdated/low quality equipment

4) Company cuts corners with low quality show teams

5) Company provides no benefits or insurance for employees

6) Company may be deeply understaffed/employees highly overworked

7) Company may not follow federal guidelines regarding labor laws (employee vs contractor fraud)

8) Company is simply not good enough to demand market rates

9) "Slow" season

10) Start-up

11) Company is struggling financially and will work for any price

So what we have is an industry that at the local and regional level competes on price with a variety of questionable at best and illegal at worst methods. Many times I've observed low price A/V providers using unskilled workers to do unsafe things while likely paying them illegally. And at the national level, the industry competes on price by knowing every possible way to cut corners while still achieving "good enough" when it comes to outcome and standards. As an A/V buyer, are you OK with that?

Remember, to practice A/V there is no requirement for training, experience, licenses, certifications, nothing. Literally anyone can practice A/V and no local, state or Federal authority provides any oversight whatsoever. The industry is self-regulated.

Because of how the A/V industry works, it is YOUR RESPONSIBILITY as a meeting planner or event producer to make sense of the quotes from different providers. That's an important and sometimes stressful job for meeting planners and event producers.

When looking at the quotes and proposals from different providers, ask yourself this: if you focus only on the extensive lists of equipment, along with "labor" hours and rates, how does that information describe what you are actually buying? What value does that list of equipment have to you? We already know that equipment doesn't equal outcome, so if provider A is charging $100 per day to rent a loudspeaker, and provider B is charging $75 per day, is provider B a better deal? Or a better value to all the stakeholders if the actual outcomes are not discussed and required? Of course, the truth is, we honestly don't know!

After decades in the industry, I can freely share that providers substitute equipment all the time. Sometimes you get better parts than you ordered; sometimes worse… Sometimes when you order a "Widget 2000" the provider had it available during the quoting stage but now it's out of stock when it comes time for your meeting. The provider has to make a choice: rent the "Widget 2000" from a competitor or substitute something that is available. I have been faced with that choice hundreds of times; deliver what we promised, but at greater internal cost or take our chances with something less expensive and hope we get "lucky" and/or no one notices. For me the decision is an easy one; deliver what was promised, or maybe better. But not everyone in the A/V business thinks that way.

If there is any "maneuvering" behind the scenes to fulfill your meeting or event, would you know? Are there any "tell-tale" signs to look for? The answer is no. If you ordered 60 "uplights" but the provider only brings and installs 58, does that even matter? Are you going to count them? If you rented microphone brand A, but the provider delivers and uses microphone brand B, would you notice? Would you care? What about generic "look-alikes" to popular A/V equipment. You order the brand name piece but the provider substitutes a "look-alike" in its place. Would you notice? Or care?

If you are a "lowest cost at any cost" shopper, do you think it's realistic to get the very best while paying the very least? If you are a "best of the best no matter what it costs" shopper, would you be OK with substitutions and shortcuts, even if they are not immediately visible?

After executing thousands of meetings and events, sending off tens of thousands of quotes, and paying attention to what matters and what doesn't, my opinion is that the buyer is really only left with three things: outcome, final (not quoted) price, and the overall experience along the way.

As an A/V buyer, it's possible to drive yourself completely insane trying to manage or micromanage the concerns mentioned in the last paragraph and throughout this book. It's also very possible (I see it all the time) to price pressure your provider into a position where they are unable to keep their promises to you. Sometimes, when faced with the pressures of running a business, and the possibility of losing a job that might keep the doors open, good providers sometimes make bad choices. Your negotiated "great deal" may put your meeting or event at great risk of failure.

All of this becomes a non-issue if you focus on outcomes, and final price, while valuing your own sanity through the process. In the end, it's up to you to decide what risks you are willing to accept vs what you choose to spend.

U.C.B.MARK'N gives you the tools to mitigate that risk on the front end and lock down your outcomes on the back end, while allowing vendors to compete on price fairly. YOU are back in the driver's seat, and as the saying goes "you follow the recipe and you'll get the dish".

Chapter 9

Non-Profit and Charities

According to the National Center for Charitable Statistics, (NCCS) there are over 1.5 MILLION registered charities in the United States. Sometimes, it can feel like every one of them calls each year with their hand out.

To be fair, the good people who volunteer their time, talent and treasures to organizations and causes that make a world a better place, they have an impossible job. And the work they do is inspiring and necessary.

With my position stated above for the record, the rest of this chapter will be mostly tough love and of course some helpful hints for working with A/V providers.

Let's start at a useful and truthful place: your cause is not my cause. Your mission is not my mission. And I or my business don't owe you ANYTHING. But that also doesn't mean I'm not willing to help! On the contrary, I might very much want to help. But virtually every person from 501C3 organizations that reach out to me, within just a few minutes, have talked themselves out of ever receiving help from me or my company.

Why is that? What is the magic formula when speaking with an A/V provider that has the best chances of getting them on board with your needs and organization?

Before I "spill the beans" so to speak, I'd like to share a story. It was a fundraising breakfast by a nationally renowned children's hospital. Their groundbreaking work is recognized around the world and is now being modeled by other similar organizations across the United States.

Attending as an invited guest, I was sitting in the "cheap seats" towards the end of the room. It was set up wide and shallow. After several moving keynotes, a video was played before the financial ask of all the guests. As the video played, everyone in the center of room was crying their eyes out watching the presentation and learning about how lives were being changed. Where I was sitting, everyone was texting, reading email, checking their watches and chatting with each other.

Four TVs were set up to show the video. The two TVs in the center of the room worked perfectly. The two TVs at the far ends of the room were blank. For whatever reason, they did not work. Half of the guests never saw the video.

What do you imagine was the financial impact of that technical faux pas? Tens of thousands of dollars? A hundred thousand dollars? The truth is we'll never know. What we do know is that the hospital, after all of its planning, left the outcome of the most important moment of its presentation to the "house" to handle and no operator or technical person was present.

It's possible that decision was made to cut costs or maybe the stakeholders just assumed that everything would work perfectly on its own.

If you are responsible for procuring A/V support for your 501C3 organization's upcoming function, ask yourself what is the one most important thing that no matter what, cannot fail. I would hope we can all agree it is the message. Not the muffins, not the chair covers, not which font looks best on the invitations, but the message. The message about the mission is what will drive the maximum amount of revenue and EVERYTHING else that happens will depend in some way on the organizations revenue.

If you only pay market rate for one thing, it should be the A/V support. Again, please appreciate where this is coming from and resist the temptation to consider the idea self-serving. Your organization is trying to drive a business outcome and needs to make sound business decisions in service of that outcome. Separate the nice-to-haves from the need-to-haves. You NEED to have a venue and you NEED to communicate your message. Everything else is a nice-to-have.

Ok, when it's time to choose an A/V support provider, begin the conversation prepared to pay market rates. And always remember, you are no different than any other customer, but you probably do have a more interesting story than most regular customers. That story, your story, is what might help you lower your costs on A/V support.

Here's what won't help you lower costs on A/V

- Holding your event on the busiest Saturday of the year in the fanciest venue in your city
- Crying broke
- "Selling" the provider on your mission
- Trying to guilt the provider
- Trying to back the provider into a corner
- Overselling "in-kinds" that have no value whatsoever (logo in the program, etc.)

So, what can you do to maximize your chances of winning a discount? Here is what I would say if I was responsible for acquiring A/V support for a 501C3 that I supported.

"Mr. A/V provider, I'm Pat with "Let's Save the Kittens" and we are planning our annual fundraiser in 6 months. You probably get lots of requests from non-

profits and they all tell you the same thing when it comes time to talk about A/V. I'm not here to ask for a hand-out and I understand you have a business to run…   With that said, is there some way we can "meet in the middle" and start a conversation about this year's event?"

What I've done is acknowledge that the provider gets lots of requests like mine and considers these conversations to be a waste of his time. I've also not tried to sell him on why my organization is so special and deserving of free stuff from him. AND, I've not promised a whole bunch of "in-kind" compensation that is not only worthless, but likely insulting if presented with a high-energy oversell of its value.

At this point, if the provider is interested in helping, he'll say so. And you as the planner or buyer can focus the conversation on outcomes while also paying special attention to what a win-win would look like for both parties.

PLEASE PLEASE PLEASE don't have this conversation three weeks before your event date. That just shows your organization to be unorganized and likely very difficult to work with!

Earlier I mentioned "backing the provider into a corner" as a tactic to avoid. Those interactions generally sound something like "Well, if you say 'no' then you're missing a HUGE opportunity… powerful influencer Mrs. Fancy McFancy Pants will be there and she's someone you want to know and there's probably no other way for you to meet her, etc…"

Because I will be working and not a guest, the actual likelihood of a meaningful conversation or even just an introduction to Mrs. McFancy Pants is very slim. The offer is a hollow one.

In summary, I acknowledge the challenges faced by 501C3 organizations when it comes to being good stewards of their treasures. And I agree that every penny counts and should be put to its best use, which is supporting the mission. But I also encourage decision makers to make good business decisions about sharing their message with maximum impact. To ask for or expect a hand out on the one thing that most impacts their financial results is small thinking. It is throwing away a dollar to save a nickel. Why would any organization choose to do that?

Chapter 10

In Show Business, Anything Can Happen

This chapter is super-short because the idea is super-simple. In show business, anything can happen. That means even the very best plans sometimes "don't survive meeting the enemy" and will need to be adjusted, adapted or even thrown out. And that's why you need a great plan, so you can pause and pivot vs panic and fail when everything gets crazy.

Far too many good, well-meaning people get themselves into trouble when it comes to A/V support for meetings and events believing they can just "figure it out" onsite or expect that the equipment will just work and everything will fall into place.

If you've ever used a computer, you know that sometimes they "act up" and require either an expert or a strong hand to get them back on track. Sometimes when you want to show a PowerPoint in your own office or a client wants to hook into the TV in your conference room, it can take longer than expected to get up and running. A/V is like that, but times 698,412,984,726,541,687,986,512.

Every piece of equipment used in your meeting or event is a potential problem and a possible failure point. I've seen $100,000 video projectors not work and after troubleshooting, the problem turned out to be a $5 adapter that failed. Modern A/V equipment is controlled by computers, uses wired and wireless networking, is bounced around in trucks to and from each job, operates on power that isn't always stable and requires really smart folks to make it all come together.

In the business we often call jobs onsite "war zones" and reference being "in the trenches" as just another day at the office. When you are ready to make your final decision selecting an A/V provider, consider above all, who you want to be "in the trenches" with, then embark on your journey with flexibility and enthusiasm and most importantly, OWN YOUR OUTCOMES.

Event well!

The end.

ABOUT THE AUTHOR

Pat Semeraro lives in Orlando, FL with his wife Cristin and cat Buddy.

www.ingramcontent.com/pod-product-compliance
Lightning Source LLC
Chambersburg PA
CBHW061201180526
45170CB00002B/903